NOBODY'S PERFECT, CHARLIE BROWN

CHARLES M. SCHULZ

Selected Cartoons from
YOU CAN DO IT, CHARLIE BROWN Vol. I

A FAWCETT CREST BOOK
Fawcett Publications, Inc., Greenwich, Conn.
Member of American Book Publishers Council, Inc.

Other PEANUTS Books in Fawcett Crest Editions:

NOBODY'S PERFECT, CHARLIE BROWN

OR WHY COULDN'T MCCOVEY HAVE HIT THE BALL EVEN **TWO** FEET HIGHER?

TO THOSE
OF US WITH
REAL
UNDERSTANDING,
DANCING
IS THE ONLY
PURE ART
FORM!